HENRIK IBSEN

Born in Norway in 1828, Ibsen began his ....
romantic history plays influenced by Shakespeare and Sch...
In 1851 he was appointed writer-in-residence at the newly
established Norwegian Theatre in Bergen with a contract to
write a play a year for five years, following which he was made
Artistic Director of the Norwegian Theatre in what is now Oslo.
In the 1860s he moved abroad to concentrate wholly on writing.
He began with two mighty verse dramas, *Brand* and *Peer Gynt*,
and in the 1870s and 1880s wrote the sequence of realistic
'problem' plays for which he is best known, among them *A
Doll's House*, *Ghosts*, *An Enemy of the People*, *Hedda Gabler*
and *Rosmersholm*. His last four plays, *The Master Builder*, *Little
Eyolf*, *John Gabriel Borkman* and *When We Dead Awaken*,
dating from his return to Norway in the 1890s, are increasingly
overlaid with symbolism. Illness forced him to retire in 1900,
and he died in 1906 after a series of crippling strokes.

RICHARD EYRE

Richard Eyre worked for ten years in regional theatre in Leicester, Edinburgh and Nottingham (where he commissioned and directed Trevor Griffiths's *Comedians*, which later transferred to London and Broadway), and then became producer of BBC TV's *Play for Today*. In London his theatre work as adapter includes his versions of Jennifer Dawson's novel *The Ha Ha*, Sartre's *Les Mains Sales*, Ibsen's *Hedda Gabler* and *Ghosts* at the Almeida Theatre and the West End. He became Artistic Director of the National Theatre in 1988, and has directed numerous productions there, including *Guys and Dolls*, *The Beggar's Opera*, *Hamlet*, *Richard III*, *King Lear*, *Night of the Iguana*, *Sweet Bird of Youth*, *Racing Demon*, *Skylight*, *The Absence of War*, *Napoli Milionaria*, *La Grande Magia*, *White Chameleon*, *The Prince's Play*, *John Gabriel Borkman*, *The Invention of Love*, *The Reporter*, *The Observer*, *Welcome to Thebes* and *Liolà*. His other theatre work includes *Hamlet*, *Edmond*, *The Shawl* and *Kafka's Dick* at the Royal Court; *Amy's View*, *The Judas Kiss*, *Mary Poppins* and *Private Lives* in the West End and on Broadway; *The Crucible* on Broadway; *The Last Cigarette* and *The Pajama Game* at Chichester and the West End; *Vincent in Brixton*, *Quartermaine's Terms*, *Betty Blue Eyes*, *Stephen Ward* and *Mr Foote's Other Leg* in the West End. His opera work includes *La traviata* at the Royal Opera House; *Manon Lescaut* at the Baden-Baden Festspielhaus; *Carmen*, *Werther* and *Le nozze di Figaro* at the Metropolitan Opera. His film and television work includes *The Imitation Game*, *Comedians*, *Country*, *The Insurance Man*, *Tumbledown*, *Suddenly Last Summer*, *The Ploughman's Lunch*, *Iris*, *Stage Beauty*, *Notes on a Scandal*, *The Other Man*, *Henry IV Part I and II*, *The Dresser* and *Changing Stages*, a six-part look at twentieth-century theatre which he wrote and presented. He has published four books, including *National Service*, a journal of his time at the National Theatre, which won the Theatre Book Prize, and *What Do I Know?*, a collection of essays about people, politics and the arts, also published by Nick Hern Books. He has received many awards for theatre, television and film, was knighted in 1997, and became a Fellow of the Royal Society of Literature in 2011.

Henrik Ibsen

LITTLE EYOLF

in a new version by
Richard Eyre

from a literal translation by
Karin and Anne Bamborough

with an Introduction by Richard Eyre

NICK HERN BOOKS
London
www.nickhernbooks.co.uk

A Nick Hern Book

This version of *Little Eyolf* first published in Great Britain in 2015 as a paperback original by Nick Hern Books Limited, The Glasshouse, 49 Goldhawk Road, London W12 8QP

This version of *Little Eyolf* by Richard Eyre copyright © 2015 Chestermead Ltd
Introduction by Richard Eyre copyright © 2015 Chestermead Ltd
This version is from a literal translation by Karin and Anne Bamborough

Richard Eyre has asserted his moral right to be identified as the author of this version

Cover photograph by John Angerson

Designed and typeset by Nick Hern Books, London
Printed in Great Britain by CPI Books (UK) Ltd

A CIP catalogue record for this book is available from the British Library

ISBN 978 1 84842 539 2

Introduction
Richard Eyre

If I said that to watch *Little Eyolf* is a terrifying experience you might think I was being histrionic, and if I said that to experience that terror is enlightening, you might think I was being pretentious. But you'd be wrong: as with Greek tragedy, you'd be seeing the white bones of human experience. You'd be looking in the face of truth, which is always a journey into light, however painful.

Imagine that your only child has drowned and the child's body is still missing. Incredulity will give way to numbness, numbness to anger, anger to despair, despair to exhaustion, exhaustion, perhaps, to acceptance, and acceptance, possibly, to hope. Add heartbreak to this – a metaphor that seems fanciful until it becomes undeniably literal – and then imagine that you and your partner don't know how to comfort each other, barely know each other, don't love each other, don't want to be with each other. That's the fate of the grieving, unloving, couple in *Little Eyolf* for whom there is no solace but each other. Tennyson's line from *In Memoriam* could serve as their epitaph: 'On the bald streets breaks the blank day'.

Grief is the anvil on which the issues – marriage, sex, class, fear of failure, fear of death, fear of life – are hammered out in Ibsen's short play. It's not, however, the sum of issues or subjects or themes, still less is it a moral primer. There are obvious poetic tropes – the rats, the deep waters of the fjord, the tops of the high mountains – but the characters are undeniably rooted in a physical world and exist entirely independently of their maker. None are constructs or symbols, not even the outlandish woman who comes to the Allmers' house offering to take care of things that 'bite and gnaw'.

As the young James Joyce said, 'Ibsen's plays contain men and women as we meet them in real life, not as we apprehend them in the world of faery.' And, as a small child in rural Dorset in the 1950s, I did meet them – the man with skin like beech bark, thick black stubble and large black eyes whose language I couldn't understand: an Italian prisoner of war looking for work; the small woman with a weasel face swathed in coloured scarves: a Gypsy selling clothes pegs. They were frightening to me, threats to the inviolability of my safe, middle-class territory.

Above all, *Little Eyolf* asks questions about marriage: how can survive it without sex, without mutual respect and without children? It was written by a sixty-six-year-old man whose thirty-six-year-old marriage had been a source of quiet unhappiness to him, and almost certainly more so to his partner. He'd returned from twenty-seven years – more than half his married life – in self-imposed exile in Italy and Germany to discover that he was revered in Kristianiana (known now as Oslo). He became a popular, if reclusive and curmudgeonly, public figure and with a remorseless lack of self-pity began to audit his life in his writing. In *The Master Builder*, which preceded *Little Eyolf*, and in *John Gabriel Borkman*, which succeeded it, he wrote of the personal landscape that he described as 'the contradiction between ability and aspiration, between will and possibility' – the conflict between love and work, between selflessness and selfishness, between comradeship and isolation, between the brightness of passion and the bleakness of unrealised emotions.

Ibsen might have said, as Chekhov did, that, 'If you are afraid of loneliness, don't get married.' Although the two writers – almost exact contemporaries – have much in common, I used to think that a liking for them both was impossible: you declared yourself for one party or the other. But the more familiar I've become with Ibsen's plays, the more I've come to think that Chekhov was speaking for both of them when he said:

It's about time for writers – particularly those who are genuine artists – to recognise that in this world you cannot figure out everything. Just have a writer who the crowds trust to be courageous enough and declare that he does not understand everything, and that alone will represent a major contribution to the way people think, a long leap forward.

Both writers were prescient about attitudes to class and to sex. The finely calibrated class distinctions in *Little Eyolf* are thoroughly recognisable in the social topography of today and you don't have to look further than the refugee detention camps at Calais to find parallels with Ibsen's feral boys on the beach and the rat-woman on the doorstep. The treatment of sex seems hardly less contemporary. It isn't buried in Freudian allegories, it's all too present in Rita's rebuke of Alfred for spurning her and in his desire for his sister, Asta. A *ménage à trois* is even suggested as a resolution of the sexual triangle. The absence of sex between husband and wife engenders hatred; its presence between brother and sister poisons love.

Little Eyolf is the godparent of many plays about marriage – Strindberg's *Dance of Death* (written six years after Eyolf), O'Neill's *Long Day's Journey Into Night*, Williams' *Cat on a Hot Tin Roof*, Albee's *Who's Afraid of Virginia Woolf?*, Whitehead's *Alpha Beta*, as well as countless TV dramas, the most recent being *Doctor Foster* and *The Affair*. It continues to exist as a play for today in much the same way as little Eyolf continues to exist for his parents. The appalling irony for them is that they recognise his humanity in death where they had ignored it in life. What remains of their son is hope – merely a glimmer of it – the hope that they will start to acknowledge their shared humanity with the dispossessed, and that their stoicism will soften into something like love.

This is the third Ibsen play that I've adapted for the Almeida Theatre. The other two, *Hedda Gabler* and *Ghosts*, were no less intense and testing than *Little Eyolf*. As with the other two plays I worked from a literal version – this time by Anne and Karen Bamborough – and had the original (Dano-Norwegian) text by my side. I was always curious about the length and sound of the original lines even if their sense was only accessible with a dictionary.

The only existing translation I looked at was an American version published in 1909, introduced and translated by the journalist and critic H. L. Menken, the great aphorist and satirist. 'It is mutual trust,' he said, 'even more than mutual interest that holds human associations together. Our friends seldom profit us but they make us feel safe. Marriage is a scheme to accomplish exactly that same end.' In his introduction to the play, he says this:

Ibsen set himself to study the influence of marriage upon human character and happiness. The things which differentiate marriage from all other forms of contract, he saw clearly enough, are its unconditionality and its unlimited duration. But does a man ever attain such complete mastery of himself as this unconditional promise implies? Is he really superior, after all, to the forces which make for evolution – the forces from which Allmers deduces his 'law of change'?

I've tried to animate the language in a way that felt as true as possible to what I understood to be the author's intentions, but even literal translations make choices and the choices we make are made according to taste, to the times we live in and how we view the world. All choices are choices of intention, of meaning. I've made a few small cuts and have replaced the three locations of the original – a 'richly furnished garden room', a 'small valley in the forest', and an 'overgrown rise in the garden' – with a single location: a veranda looking out over the fjord. What I have written is a 'version' or 'adaptation' or 'interpretation' of Ibsen's play, but I hope that it comes close to squaring the circle of being close to what Ibsen intended while seeming spontaneous to an audience of today.

This version of *Little Eyolf* was first performed at the
Almeida Theatre, London, on 26 November 2015
(previews from 19 November), with the following cast:

ALFRED ALLMERS	Jolyon Coy
BJARNE BORGHEIM	Sam Hazeldine
RITA ALLMERS	Lydia Leonard
ASTA ALLMERS	Eve Ponsonby
WOMAN	Eileen Walsh
EYOLF	Adam Greaves-Neal
	Tom Hibberd
	Billy Marlow

Director	Richard Eyre
Designer	Tim Hatley
Lighting Designer	Peter Mumford
Sound Designer	John Leonard
Projection Designer	Jon Driscoll
Casting Director	Cara Beckinsale
Assistant Director	Sara Joyce
Company Stage Manager	Laura Draper

'On the bald streets breaks the blank day'
Tennyson: In Memoriam

Characters

ALFRED ALLMERS, *writer, thirty-six*
RITA ALLMERS, *his wife, thirty*
EYOLF, *their son, nine*
ASTA ALLMERS, *Alfred's half-sister, twenty-five*
BJARNE BORGHEIM, *civil engineer, thirty*
WOMAN, *rat-catcher, forty-five*

This text went to press before the end of rehearsals and so may differ slightly from the play as performed.

*Early-morning mist. Through the mist we see the sun start
slowly to burn through.*

*The sun merges into water – the surface of a fjord. The calm
surface dissolves into a whirlpool.*

*The image of water dissolves into the view of a narrow fjord
banked by wooded hillsides.*

*It's morning in early summer. The sun shines warmly on an
elegant veranda – a deck without railings. It's a wealthy house:
varnished wood and Norwegian red. On one side there's a
round outdoor table flanked by two chairs; on the other side
there's a sort of chaise longue/sunbed with rich cushions and
rugs. By the chaise there's a small coffee table. There are steps
which go down, out of view, from the veranda towards the fjord.
There's a door to the house on one side, open French windows.*

*A dark-haired young woman is standing with her back to the
fjord, unpacking a large rucksack that's on the table. She takes
papers out, examining them as she does so. The young woman
is* RITA. *She's about thirty, good-looking, voluptuous almost.
She's dressed in a white dressing gown and is barefoot.*

ASTA *comes up the steps from the fjord, wearing a summer
dress, with hat and jacket. She's twenty-five, slim, medium
height, with light hair and deep, earnest eyes. She carries a
largish shoulder bag.*

She watches RITA *silently for a few moments, then speaks
quietly.*

ASTA. Rita –

RITA (*jumping*). Asta! What are you doing here?

ASTA. I felt so restless, I thought I just had to see how Eyolf
was. And you. So I took the ferry and...

*She shrugs as if to say 'here I am', then takes off her hat and
jacket and puts them on the sofa beside the door. She lays
her bag on the table beside the sofa.*

RITA (*smiling*). And I suppose you met a 'friend' on board? Pure coincidence, of course.

ASTA. I didn't see anyone. What's that?

RITA. Alfred's bag. Don't you recognise it?

ASTA. Is Alfred back?

RITA. Late last night.

ASTA. So *that's* what must have drawn me out here. He hadn't let you know?

RITA *shakes her head and continues to take things out of the bag.*

Not even a postcard?

RITA. Not even a postcard.

ASTA. He didn't send a telegram?

RITA. An hour before he arrived. (*Laughing.*) Typical, no?

ASTA. Well, he's always kept everything to himself.

RITA. But it made it better to have him home again...

ASTA. I'm sure...

RITA. ...because I hadn't expected him for a fortnight.

ASTA. He's not, um, depressed?

RITA *closes the bag with a snap and smiles at* ASTA.

RITA. He stood there as if he'd had a revelation.

ASTA. Wasn't he tired?

RITA. Shattered. He'd walked most of the way, poor thing.

ASTA. Perhaps he'd got a cold on the walk.

RITA. I haven't heard him cough once.

ASTA. Well, there you are, the doctor was right to make him go walking in the mountains.

RITA. Well, it's been awful for me, I didn't want to talk about it and anyway you hardly ever came to see me –

ASTA. I'm sorry, I –

RITA. Of course you had your *teaching*, but your road-digger was away, you could have –

ASTA. Rita...

RITA. All right, don't let's talk about the 'engineer'. You can't believe how much I've missed Alfred. The house felt so sad, it was as if somebody had died.

ASTA. It's only been a few weeks...

RITA. We've never been apart before, not even for a day, not once in ten years.

ASTA. But that's exactly why it was time for him to have a bit of an outing. He ought to go hiking every summer.

RITA *shakes her head, half-smiling.*

No, I mean it, Rita.

RITA. Well, it's all very well for you to talk. If I was like you, perhaps I'd have let him go before, but I couldn't, I've always thought I'd never get him back again. Can't you understand that?

ASTA. No I can't. Maybe it's because I have no one to lose.

RITA. Really?

ASTA. Not that I know of. Is Alfred still in bed?

RITA. He got up as early as he always does.

ASTA. So he can't have been so shattered after all.

RITA. He was when he arrived, but he's been with Eyolf in his room for at least an hour.

ASTA. Is Eyolf always going to be studying?

RITA (*with a shrug*). That's what Alfred wants.

ASTA. But you don't have to go along with it.

RITA. I can't interfere. He knows much more about these things than I do and anyway what else can Eyolf do? He can't run around like other children.

ASTA. I'm going to talk to Alfred about it.

RITA. Well, do. Look –

ALFRED ALLMERS, *dressed in a linen summer suit, comes in from the house. He's a lightly built man of about thirty-six with a serious expression and thin brown hair and beard. He's holding the hand of his nine-year-old son,* EYOLF, *who wears a sort of military uniform – some gold braid and buttons, but it's the uniform of a fighter not a toy soldier.*

EYOLF *is small for his age and delicate, but has very intelligent eyes. One of his legs is shrunken and he walks with an improvised wooden support – half-stick, half-crutch.*

As soon as ALFRED *sees* ASTA, *he drops* EYOLF's *hand, goes to her, and embraces her.*

ALFRED. Asta, darling Asta! Imagine you being here, I never thought I'd see you so soon.

ASTA. I felt I had to… Welcome home!

ALFRED (*kissing her cheeks*). Thank you for coming.

RITA. Doesn't he look good?

ASTA. Wonderful… wonderful. You look so much better. You must have done so much writing when you were away. Have you finished the book, Alfred?

ALFRED. Oh, the book…

ASTA. I knew you'd find it easy once you got away.

ALFRED. I thought so too, but that's not how it turned out. To be honest, I haven't written a word.

ASTA. Not a word?

RITA. That explains all those blank pages in your bag.

ASTA. Then what have you been doing?

ALFRED (*smiles*). Thinking and thinking and thinking –

RITA *takes his arm and puts it round her neck.*

RITA. Of those you'd left at home?

ALFRED. Yes of course. A lot. Every day.

RITA. Then everything's fine.

RITA *takes his arm away, smiling.*

ASTA. You haven't written a word but you look so, I don't know... content. You usually look so depressed when your work's going badly.

ALFRED. Yes, but I've been an idiot before. The thinking is what matters, what you write isn't important.

ASTA. What?

RITA. Don't be so ridiculous, Alfred.

EYOLF. What you write *is* important, Papa.

ALFRED *smiles and strokes* EYOLF's *hair.*

ALFRED. If you say so, but there'll be someone who'll do it better. As the Bible says: 'There cometh one mightier than I after me.'

EYOLF. Who?

ALFRED. Just wait. We'll hear about him soon.

EYOLF. And what will you do then?

ALFRED. Go to the mountains again...

RITA. Don't be absurd.

ALFRED....up to the high peaks and the great white spaces.

EYOLF. Can I come with you?

ALFRED. Perhaps.

EYOLF. It would be so wonderful, you know, to go climbing with you.

ASTA. You're brilliantly dressed today, Eyolf.

EYOLF. Do you think so, Auntie?

ASTA. Of course I do. Is it for your papa?

EYOLF. Mama let me dress up for him.

ALFRED (*aside to* RITA). You shouldn't have let him dress like that.

RITA (*sotto voce*). He set his heart on the uniform, went on and on about it...

EYOLF. Oh, I haven't told you, Papa, Bjarne bought me a bow.

ALFRED (*to* RITA). Bjarne?

RITA. He means Borgheim.

EYOLF. He's taught me how to use it too.

ALFRED. Oh that's wonderful, Eyolf.

EYOLF. And next time he comes, I'm going to ask him to teach me to swim.

ALFRED. Why do you want to learn to swim?

EYOLF. All the boys down at the beach can swim, I'm the only one that can't.

ALFRED *puts his arms round* EYOLF.

ALFRED. You can learn whatever you want.

EYOLF. Do you know what I want most of all, Papa?

ALFRED. No I don't.

EYOLF. I want to join the army.

ALFRED. Oh, Eyolf, there are so many, better things to do.

EYOLF. But I'll have to join the army when I grow up, won't I?

ALFRED. Well... yes. Yes... well, we'll see.

ASTA *sits at the table*.

ASTA. Eyolf, come here and I'll tell you something.

EYOLF *goes to her*. RITA *is sitting on the chaise*.

EYOLF. What is it, Auntie?

ASTA. Guess who I've seen?

EYOLF. Who?

ASTA. Do you know, Eyolf, I've seen the rat-woman.

EYOLF. The rat-woman? You're joking.

ASTA. No, it's true, I saw her yesterday.

EYOLF. Where?

ASTA. On the road, outside the town.

ALFRED. I saw her, too. In the country.

RITA. Perhaps it'll be our turn next, Eyolf.

EYOLF (*to* ASTA). Don't you think it's weird that she's called the rat-woman?

ASTA. People call her the rat-woman because she goes round the country getting rid of rats.

ALFRED. I've heard her real name is Lupus.

EYOLF. That's Latin for wolf.

ALFRED. You know so much, Eyolf.

EYOLF *goes to* ALFRED.

EYOLF. Do you think... at night... that she might turn into... a werewolf?

ALFRED. No. No, I don't think so. Now why don't you go and play.

EYOLF. Don't I have to do more homework?

ALFRED. No no, you can play on the beach with the other boys.

EYOLF. I don't want to.

ALFRED. Why not?

EYOLF. Cos of these clothes.

ALFRED. Do they make fun of... of your clothes?

EYOLF. They don't dare, I'd beat them up if they did.

ALFRED. Well then, why?

EYOLF. They say I can't ever be a soldier.

ALFRED. Why do they say that?

EYOLF. They're jealous cos they don't have any money. They go around barefoot.

ALFRED (*to* RITA). He just tears my heart apart…

   RITA *rises to calm* ALFRED.

RITA. Alfred…

ALFRED. These little bastards'll soon learn.

ASTA. Ssssh –

   They all stop and listen. They hear a tapping.

   There's someone tapping.

EYOLF. It must be Bjarne.

   As they listen a small, thin, ageless WOMAN *who looks like a tinker appears from the steps. She has sharp, piercing eyes and nut-brown skin, and is wearing an old-fashioned flowered dress, with a black hood and cloak. She's holding a large red umbrella, and a black bag looped over her arm.*

   She's the WOMAN *known as the 'rat-woman'.*

   EYOLF *runs to* ASTA, *clutching her skirt.*

   As the WOMAN *comes onto the veranda, she curtsies. She speaks in a very broad (Irish) dialect.*

WOMAN. Begging pardon, but would the master and mistress be bothered by any things that bites and gnaws in the house?

ALFRED (*bemused*). Things that bite? No, I don't think so.

WOMAN. It would be a pleasure to rid your worships' house of them, so it would.

RITA. We don't have anything like that here.

WOMAN. That's unlucky, that's bad cess. I just happened to be on me rounds now and god alone knows when I'll be in these parts again. (*Mutters.*) *Marbh tuirseach.* [*Dead tired.*]

   The WOMAN *looks as though she might collapse.* ALFRED *rather reluctantly indicates the chaise.*

ALFRED. You look tired.

WOMAN. You never get tired of doing good to the poor craiters that are so persecuted but it takes the strength out of you, so it does.

RITA. Won't you sit down and rest a little?

WOMAN. Thank you, thank you, your ladyship.

She sits, putting down her umbrella and the bag that she's been carrying.

I've been at my work all night.

ALFRED. Have you really?

WOMAN. Over on the islands. (*Cackling.*) Those people sent for me, you know. They didn't like it but it had to be done and they had to put a good face on it and bite the bitter apple.

She looks at EYOLF and nods.

The bitter apple, little master, the bitter apple.

EYOLF. Why did they have to...?

WOMAN. What?

EYOLF. To bite it?

WOMAN. Because they couldn't keep body and soul together on account of the rats and all their baby rats, young master.

RITA (*to EYOLF*). They were poor, you see. (*To the WOMAN.*) And were there so many rats?

WOMAN. Swarming with them, it was. (*Laughing gleefully.*) They crept and crawled into beds all night long and plopped into the milk churns and went criss-crossing, pittering and pattering, all over the floors.

EYOLF (*whispering to ASTA*). I don't ever want to go there.

WOMAN. But then I came along. And I took another with me. And we persuaded all of the little darlings to come with us and then we made an end of every single one of them.

EYOLF (*screaming*). Look!

RITA. Oh, for God's sake, Eyolf.

ALFRED. What's the matter?

EYOLF *points at the* WOMAN*'s bag. There's something alive in it: a rat?*

EYOLF. There's something wriggling in the bag.

RITA (*shrieks*). Get rid of her, Alfred!

WOMAN (*laughing*). Oh, my lady, you needn't be scared of such a little mannikin.

ALFRED. What is it?

WOMAN. It's only little Mopseyman.

She loosens the string of the bag and a small dog with a black snout, pokes its head out. She talks softly to it.

Come up out of the dark, dotey, come on alanna.

She nods to EYOLF, *beckons to him.*

Come along, don't be afraid, my little wounded soldier, he won't bite. Come here... come here...

EYOLF *clings to* ASTA.

EYOLF. I don't want to.

WOMAN. Don't you think Mopsey has a sweet and gentle face, young master?

EYOLF. Him?

WOMAN. Yes, him.

EYOLF. He's got the most horrible face I've ever seen.

She closes the bag.

WOMAN. Give it time, give it time... you'll change your mind, dearie...

EYOLF *is involuntarily drawn to the* WOMAN. *He strokes the bag cautiously.*

But now he's a wheen tired and weary, poor mite. He's banjaxed, so he is.

EYOLF. Lovely... he's lovely...

WOMAN (*to* ALFRED). The game takes the strength out of you, sir.

ALFRED. What game?

WOMAN. Follow me leader.

ALFRED. Do you mean the rats follow the dog?

WOMAN. Mopseyman and I do it together. Easiest thing in the world, I just slip a string through his collar and lead him three times round a house and play on my panpipes and when they hear that, they come up from the cellars and down from the lofts and out of their boles, all of them, bless them.

EYOLF. Does he bite them to death?

WOMAN. Not at all, not at all. We go to the boat, he and I do... and then they do follow after us, the big squealers and the little ratikins.

EYOLF. And then what? What happens?

WOMAN. Then we push out from the shore and I scull with one oar and play on my panpipes and Mopseyman swims behind and all the crawlers and creepers and scrabblers and tearers follow us out into the deep... into the deep waters. They *have* to, you see.

EYOLF. Why do they have to?

WOMAN. Because they don't want to. Because they're so *scanraithe*...

They look baffled.

...so *frightened* of the shallow water that they have to go to the deep.

EYOLF. Are they drowned, then?

WOMAN. Every last one. (*Whispering.*) And there they are, still and peaceful and dark as their hearts can desire, the lovely little angels. They sleep a long, sweet sleep down there with no one to persecute them any more.

She stands.

In the old days, I can tell you, I didn't need any Mopseyman,
I did the tempting myself – all alone.

EYOLF. Did you tempt rats?

WOMAN. Men. One in particular.

EYOLF. Tell me who it was. Go on.

WOMAN. It was my own sweetheart.

EYOLF *looks doubtful. He looks back at his parents for
confirmation.*

(*Laughing.*) It was, my little ladykiller…

EYOLF. And where is he now?

WOMAN. He's down in the deep with all the other rats.

She starts to get her things together.

I must be off and get to work. (*To* RITA.) So your ladyship
has no use for me today? If you do, I could do the job right
away.

RITA. No, thank you, I don't think we'll need any of your
services.

WOMAN. Well, you never can tell. If you should find that there
is anything that keeps biting and tearing and nibbling and
crawling, then just get hold of me and Mopseyman.
Goodbye, goodbye, goodbye to all of you.

*She curtsies to them all and goes down the steps from the
veranda.*

Silence.

EYOLF (*whispering to* ASTA). Now I've seen her too.

RITA *goes to the side of the veranda and walks up and down,
fanning herself with her handkerchief.* ALFRED *goes to the
sofa table, where* ASTA *had left her bag. He picks it up.*

ALFRED. Is this yours, Asta?

As ASTA *goes to* ALFRED, EYOLF *hobbles to the veranda
steps, unnoticed, and climbs down the steps, out of view.*

ASTA. Yes. I've brought some of the letters that you asked me to sort out.

ALFRED *strokes her hair.*

ALFRED. Did you find anything interesting in them?

ASTA. There's always something interesting in family papers. (*Whispering.*) I've got Mother's letters here.

ALFRED. You must keep them.

ASTA. I need you to look at them, Freddie. Not now but...

ALFRED. I'm not going to read your mother's letters.

She looks straight at him.

ASTA. Some time when we're alone together, I'm going to tell you what's in them.

ALFRED. Yes, but you have to keep them, you haven't much to remember your mother by.

He hands ASTA *her bag. She takes it and lays it on the chair under her coat.* RITA *turns back from the edge of the veranda.*

RITA. Eeuchh... that vile woman smelt of corpses. She made me feel sick.

ALFRED. She's a bit sinister but I can understand what she was talking about when she talked about the deep waters. Being alone on the top of a mountain or on those great snow deserts has the same sort of strange power.

ASTA. What's happened to you, Alfred?

ALFRED. Happened?

ASTA. You've changed. Rita noticed it too.

RITA. I saw it straight away, but it's good, isn't it, Alfred?

ALFRED. It ought to be good. It must be good.

RITA. Something happened to you. Don't deny it. I can see it.

ALFRED. Nothing happened *to* me, but...

RITA. But what?

ALFRED. Something happened *in* me. A sort of revolution.

RITA. Oh, for God's sake…

He pats her shoulder. She avoids him and sits on the chaise.

ALFRED. It's only for the good, Rita, you can be sure of that.

RITA. You have to tell us everything now. I mean everything.

ALFRED. Asta, you should hear this too.

RITA sits on the sofa, beckoning to ALFRED to sit by her. ALFRED takes a chair from the table for ASTA and then sits on the sofa by RITA's side.

There's a silence.

RITA. Well…?

ALFRED. When I think about the last ten or eleven years, it seems to me almost like a fairytale. Or a dream. Don't you think so too, Asta?

ASTA. Yes, I do think so.

ALFRED. When I think that we were two poor orphaned children –

RITA. Oh, not that again…

ALFRED. And now I live in comfort and luxury. I'm free to study in the way that I'd always dreamed of. And all this, this astonishing good fortune we owe to you.

He holds out his hand to RITA who slaps it away half-playfully, half-angrily.

RITA. I wish you'd stop talking like that.

ALFRED. It's only a preamble…

RITA. Then skip the preamble.

ALFRED. I didn't go up to the mountains because of the doctor's advice.

ASTA. Didn't you?

RITA. Why did you go then?

ALFRED. I found I couldn't write here.

RITA. What was stopping you?

ALFRED. Nothing. No one. I just had the feeling that I was wasting or maybe... abusing whatever talent I had. Just letting the time dribble away.

ASTA. By writing?

ALFRED. I can't imagine that writing's the only thing I can do in my life. There must be something else.

RITA. Was that what you were brooding about when you were up the mountain?

ALFRED. Mostly, yes.

RITA. And that's why you've been so miserable lately and made the rest of us miserable too.

He protests.

You have, Alfred.

ALFRED. Day after day, often half the night too, I've sat bent over my desk working on that great... slab of a book. *The Responsibility of Being Human.* Huh!

ASTA. But, Freddie, that's your life's work.

RITA. Yes, that's what you keep saying, Asta.

ALFRED. That's what I thought. Ever since I grew up, that's what I've thought. It was you that made it possible for me to do it...

RITA. Oh, rubbish!

ALFRED. ...you, with 'your burnished gold and your great green forests'...

RITA. If you start all that drivel again, I'll hit you.

ASTA. But what about the book?

ALFRED. It started to... I don't know... drift away from me and other things became more and more important.

RITA. Alfred…

RITA takes ALFRED*'s hand and kisses his palm.*

ALFRED. I mean Eyolf.

RITA. Oh, Eyolf.

She drops his hand.

ALFRED. He's taken a deeper and deeper hold on me. After that awful fall and especially now we know that he can never be better –

RITA. But you do everything you can for him!

ALFRED. As a teacher, yes, but not as a father. I want to be a father to Eyolf.

RITA. I don't think I quite understand you.

ALFRED *stands and paces.*

ALFRED. I mean that I'll try everything I can to make his life as painless and as easy as it can possibly be.

RITA. Oh, but I don't think Eyolf feels it very deeply, thank God.

ASTA. He does, Rita.

ALFRED. Yes, he does feel it. Very deeply.

RITA. But what on earth do you imagine you can do for him?

ALFRED. I want to try to bring out all his potential, all the ideas that are… germinating in his young imagination. I want to nurture all the shoots of talent in him, to make them blossom and bear fruit. But I want to do more than that. I want to help him to reconcile himself to reality because everything he wants now he can't achieve but even so… even so, I want to make him happy.

He paces up and down the veranda. ASTA *and* RITA *watch him.*

RITA. You should calm down, Alfred.

ALFRED. If he wants to, Eyolf will carry on my life's work or he'll write something that's altogether his own. Maybe that'd be best. Anyway, I'm not going to write any more.

RITA *gets up and goes to* ALFRED, *who shies away from her.* RITA *turns her back and looks out over the fjord.*

RITA. Can't you work for the two of you?

ALFRED. No, I can't. I can't split myself in half, so I've got to give up writing for Eyolf. He'll be the one who'll fulfil my ambitions and my life's work will be to achieve that.

ASTA *gets up and goes to him.*

ASTA. This must have been really hard for you.

ALFRED. Yes, it was. I'd have been too weak if I'd stayed here, I could never have forced myself to renounce everything. Not here. Never.

RITA. You had to go away?

ALFRED. *Yes!* I climbed up into a world of absolute solitude. I saw the sun rise on the tops of the mountains and I felt myself nearer to the stars, as if I, as if I could... as if I was in harmony with them. That's how I was able to do it.

ASTA. You'll never write any more of your book?

ALFRED. I can't split up my life in two. I'm going to demonstrate the 'responsibility of being human' in my own life.

RITA. And do you really think you can live up to your lofty ideals?

He holds out his hands to RITA *and to* ASTA.

ALFRED. With you to help me, I can. And you too, Asta.

ASTA *takes his hand.* RITA *refuses hers.*

RITA. Oh, so you *can* divide yourself after all.

ALFRED. Oh, Rita...

RITA *turns away from him sharply and looks out over the fjord. There's a light and rapid knock on the doorway.* BJARNE BORGHEIM *enters quickly from the house. He's around thirty, a civil engineer from a working-class background. He seems confident and cheerful.* RITA *turns to him.*

BORGHEIM. Good morning, Mrs Allmers.

> *He goes towards her to shake hands but stops when he sees* ALFRED.

You're home already?

ALFRED (*shaking hands*). I came back last night.

RITA. He wasn't allowed to stay any longer, Mr Borgheim.

ALFRED. She's teasing me.

RITA. It's true, your leave of absence had expired.

BORGHEIM. You keep your husband on a tight rein.

RITA. I stand up for my rights and, anyway, everything has to end some time.

BORGHEIM. Not everything, I hope. Morning, Miss Allmers.

ASTA (*offhand*). Good morning.

RITA. You said 'not everything'?

BORGHEIM. Yes, I'm sure there's *something* that never ends.

RITA. You're thinking of love and that sort of stuff.

BORGHEIM. Well, I'm thinking of everything that's lovely.

RITA. And beauty, does that not come to an end? Oh, let's all hope for that.

ALFRED. Well, your road'll be coming to an end soon.

BORGHEIM. Finished yesterday. (*To* RITA.) Yes, true, that has come to an end.

RITA. And is that why you're looking so cocky this morning?

BORGHEIM. Am I?

RITA. Yes you are and I have to say…

BORGHEIM. What?

RITA. I don't think it's particularly polite of you, Mr Borgheim.

BORGHEIM. Why not?

RITA. Because it means we won't be seeing much of you any more.

BORGHEIM. Oh yes, I suppose it does.

RITA. But you'll be able to visit us now and then.

BORGHEIM. I'm afraid that I won't be able to do that for a long time.

ALFRED. Why?

BORGHEIM. Because I've just been offered a new contract that starts straight away.

ALFRED *shakes* BORGHEIM*'s hand.*

ALFRED. I'm so glad to hear it.

RITA. Hooray!

BORGHEIM. Ssshhh… I shouldn't have mentioned it but I couldn't stop myself. It's an amazing piece of engineering – in the north – a road through sheer mountain passes. Incredibly difficult.

He stamps his feet in joy.

What a wonderful world this is, and how wonderful to be an engineer!

RITA. And is it just road-making that's put you in such a good mood?

BORGHEIM. No, no, it's everything about the future.

RITA. Ah-ha, then maybe you've got something even more alluring in mind.

BORGHEIM. Maybe. As they say – (*Sings.*) 'when happiness comes, it often comes like a flood in spring'… (*Turning a little formally to* ASTA.) Miss Allmers, would you like to go on our usual walk?

ASTA. Um, no. No thank you. Not now. Not today.

BORGHEIM. Oh, come on, only a stroll, I've something I need to talk to you about.

RITA. Something else that you shouldn't mention?

BORGHEIM. Well...

RITA. There's nothing to stop you whispering, you know. (*Stage whisper*.) Asta, you have to go with him.

ASTA. Rita –

BORGHEIM. Asta, *Miss* Asta, please... it'll be our last walk for God knows how long.

ASTA. All right, let's walk on the beach.

BORGHEIM. Thank you, thank you so much.

ASTA puts on her hat, picks up her parasol and puts the strap of her bag over her shoulder.

ALFRED. While you're there you can see what Eyolf's up to.

BORGHEIM. Oh, I've got something for him.

ALFRED. He's playing somewhere.

BORGHEIM. Really? He's usually indoors with his homework.

ALFRED. I'm stopping that now, he has to spend his time out of doors.

BORGHEIM. Of *course* he should, he ought to be playing games in the open air all the time. We all should, after all, life's one long game, isn't it? Come along, Asta –

Miss Asta.

BORGHEIM and ASTA go down the veranda steps towards the beach. ALFRED stands looking after them.

ALFRED. Do you think there's anything actually going on between those two?

RITA. Maybe... I used to think there was but... I don't know, I don't understand her, she's become a stranger.

ALFRED. While I've been away?

RITA. In the last week or two.

ALFRED. And you think she's not interested in him now?

RITA. Not in the way you mean, no. Would it upset you if she was?

ALFRED. It wouldn't exactly upset me. But it'd certainly be worrying.

RITA. Worrying?

ALFRED. Well, you know I'm responsible for Asta's happiness.

RITA. Oh, come on, 'responsible'? She's a grown-up, she can make her own mind up.

ALFRED. Of course…

RITA. And he's not uninteresting…

ALFRED. No, I agree, quite the opposite –

RITA.… in fact, I'd be very happy if he and Asta were to marry.

ALFRED. Oh, why's that?

RITA. Because then she'd have to go away with him, a long way away, and never come here.

ALFRED. You want Asta to go away?

RITA. Yes. Yes, of course.

ALFRED. Why?

RITA. Because then I'd have you to myself at last even if we still wouldn't be *alone*.

RITA *throws her arms round his neck and starts to sob uncontrollably.*

I can't give you up.

ALFRED. Oh, Rita, be sensible…

RITA. I don't care a damn about being sensible, I only care for you. You're the only thing I care for in the whole world.

ALFRED *detaches himself, but she throws her arms round his neck again.*

I want you, I want *you*!

ALFRED. Let me go, Rita…

RITA. I want you!

ALFRED. Get off, you're strangling me...

She lets him go.

RITA. I wish I could. If you only knew how I've hated you...

ALFRED. Hated me?

RITA....when you were shut up in your room brooding over your work, long, long, long into the night, never coming to bed. How I hated you.

ALFRED. Well, now that's over.

RITA. Huh! Now you've given yourself up to something worse.

ALFRED. Something worse? Is Eyolf 'something worse'?

RITA. Yes, because he comes between you and me. The book wasn't a living thing but he is, and I won't put up with it. I won't, I'm telling you.

ALFRED. You frighten me.

RITA. I frighten myself. Don't make me do bad things.

ALFRED. Do I do that?

RITA. When you destroy what's most sacred between us.

ALFRED *starts to protest.*

Yes you do.

ALFRED. It's your own child, our only child, that you're talking about.

RITA. Half mine.

ALFRED. What?

RITA. I said he's half mine, but I want you to be entirely mine, mine entirely. It's my right.

ALFRED. Rita, it's no use demanding, things have to be given freely.

RITA. And you can't do that any more?

ALFRED. I've got to divide myself between you and Eyolf.

RITA. What if he'd never been born?

ALFRED. Well, then it would be different, I'd only have you to care for.

RITA. Then I wish he'd never been born.

ALFRED. You can't say that, Rita.

RITA. It was unbearably painful bringing him into the world but I put up with it for your sake.

ALFRED. Yes, I know, I know...

RITA. But that's got to end, I want to *live*. I don't want to be just a mother: '*Eyolf's mother*'. I won't, I'm telling you, I can't, I want to be everything to you.

ALFRED. That's what you are, through our child –

RITA. 'Through our child' – what a feeble, vapid... nauseating phrase. I won't be put off like that, I was made to bear your child but not to be his mother. You have to take me as I am, Alfred.

Silence. A distant sound of boys playing on the beach.

ALFRED. You used to love Eyolf.

RITA. I was sorry for him because... because you showed so little interest in him. You made him grind away at his schoolwork. You were hardly aware of him.

ALFRED. No, I was blind, I hadn't yet realised –

RITA. But now, I suppose, you do?

ALFRED. Yes, I do. I see now that the most important thing for me in the world is to be a proper father to Eyolf.

RITA. And what will you be to me?

ALFRED. I'll always care for you. With all the tenderness I can.

He tries to take her hands but she avoids him, swerving away.

RITA. I don't want your tenderness, I want you, the way I had you when we first knew each other and I'll never agree to being fobbed off with leftovers. *Never!*

ALFRED. I'd have thought there was enough happiness for the three of us.

RITA. Then you're easy to please.

She sits at the table.

Listen.

ALFRED. What?

RITA. When I got your telegram yesterday evening I took off all my clothes and I let my hair down...

ALFRED....your hair?...

RITA....so that it flowed down over my neck and my shoulders and my breasts...

ALFRED....yes, you looked...

RITA....and I was naked. I put rose-coloured silk over both the lamps and then I put on this dressing gown...

ALFRED....yes...

RITA....and you arrived and we were alone, just the two of us, the only people in the whole house still awake. And I'd put champagne on the table, an ice bucket, and two glasses –

ALFRED. I didn't drink any of it.

RITA. No, you didn't. Do you remember that poem: 'There stood the champagne, but he tasted it not'?

She gets up from the chair and goes over to the chaise longue like a sleepwalker and lies down on it. ALFRED stares at her.

ALFRED. I needed to talk to you about Eyolf.

RITA. And you did.

ALFRED. I didn't. You took off your dressing gown.

RITA. And you talked about little Eyolf. You wanted to know all about his digestion...

ALFRED. Rita...

RITA....and then you got into bed and went soundly to sleep.

ALFRED (*shaking his head*). Rita... Rita...

RITA. Alfred?

She stretches, then undoes her dressing gown and bares her body. She looks up at him. He's silent.

'There stood the champagne, but he tasted it not.'

Neither of them move.

ALFRED. He tasted it not.

He goes away from her and stands on the edge of the veranda. RITA *lies still, her eyes closed. Suddenly she jumps up, tying her dressing gown.*

RITA. You know something, Alfred?

ALFRED. What?

RITA. You shouldn't take me for granted.

ALFRED. Take you for granted?

RITA. You shouldn't be so sure of me.

ALFRED. What are you talking about?

RITA. I've never ever been unfaithful to you, I've never even thought of it for a moment...

ALFRED. No, I know that...

RITA.... but if you turn your back on me...

ALFRED. What d'you mean?

RITA....I don't know what I might do.

She stops suddenly. He looks at her questioningly.

If I ever thought that you didn't love me the way you used to.

ALFRED. But people change... it happens to everyone, we change.

RITA. 'It's a law, like gravity', that's what you say, isn't it? Well, I don't change and I won't have you changing either. I want you all to myself.

ALFRED. Possessiveness is a flaw in your character, Rita.

RITA (*sarcastic*). A flaw in my character? I am what I am and if anyone comes between us...

She looks at him threateningly.

ALFRED. What?

RITA. Then I'll take my revenge on you.

ALFRED. How will you 'take your revenge'?

RITA. I don't know. No, actually, I do know.

ALFRED. Well?

RITA. I'll abandon you.

ALFRED. Abandon me?

RITA. I'll throw myself at the first man I meet.

ALFRED. You'd never do that, Rita. You're too proud and you're too loyal.

She puts her arms round his neck.

RITA. Oh, you don't know what I could do if you... if you didn't want me any more.

ALFRED. How can you say that?

Half-laughing, she lets him go.

RITA. Maybe I'll cast my net for that... for the road-digger.

ALFRED. You're joking.

RITA. No I'm not. He'd do.

ALFRED. I think he's spoken for.

RITA. So much the better, I can take him away from someone else. That's exactly what Eyolf's done to me.

ALFRED. Are you accusing Eyolf?

She points at him.

RITA. You see: the moment you mention Eyolf's name, you go all soft and tearful.

She clenches her fists, as if she'd hit him.

You make me want to –

She stops herself.

ALFRED. What?

RITA. I'm not going to tell you.

She breaks away from him. He follows her.

ALFRED. Rita, you've got the devil in you.

RITA *turns her back on him, at the side of the veranda. She barely turns when* BORGHEIM *and* ASTA *come up the steps from the garden. They both look depressed, hardly suppressing their feelings.*

BORGHEIM. Well, we've had our last walk together.

RITA *(not turning)*. Oh, are you no longer 'walking out' together?

BORGHEIM. No, we're not.

RITA *(turning)*. Do you hear that, Alfred? *(To* BORGHEIM.*)* I bet it's the devil that's done this.

BORGHEIM. The devil?

RITA. Yes, the devil.

BORGHEIM. Do you believe in the devil?

RITA. Oh yes, I believe in the devil. Specially little devils.

ALFRED *(whispers)*. Rita…

RITA *(whispers)*. You make me like this.

In the distance, screams and shouts can be heard from the beach. BORGHEIM *and* ASTA *go to the edge of the veranda.* ALFRED *stays with* RITA, *their argument wholly unresolved.*

BORGHEIM. What's happening?

ASTA. Look at all those people running along the jetty.

ALFRED. It's probably those brats making trouble again.

BORGHEIM *goes halfway down the steps and shouts down.*

BORGHEIM. What's happening?

Several voices are heard answering indistinctly.

I can't hear you! What?

He goes down the steps and shouts to the beach. ASTA *follows him. We can't quite make out the words. Then* BORGHEIM *and* ASTA *come back up the steps and stand on the edge of the veranda.*

RITA. What's happened?

BORGHEIM. Someone's drowned.

ALFRED. Drowned?

ASTA. A child.

ALFRED. Oh, they can all swim.

RITA (*screams*). Where's Eyolf?

ALFRED. Rita, shush, ssshh, Eyolf's playing in the garden.

ASTA. No, he was on the beach.

RITA (*in agony*). Oh… oh…

RITA *is contorted with pain. More indistinct voices are heard.* BORGHEIM *and* ASTA *rush down the steps.*

ALFRED. It isn't Eyolf, Rita, it couldn't be him –

RITA. *SHUT UP, LET ME LISTEN!*

She goes to the edge of the veranda, craning to hear. Indistinct voices float up. Then she comes back to ALFRED, *a walking ghost.*

ALFRED. What are they saying?

RITA. 'There's a stick floating…'

ALFRED (*shaking his head violently*). No… no… no…

RITA. You have to save him, you have to –

ALFRED. I have to save him...

He rushes down the steps. RITA *remains motionless, turned away from the fjord.*

The view of the fjord becomes the whirlpool and at the centre of the whirlpool is EYOLF's *body turning in the vortex. The water becomes still and* EYOLF's *body can be seen floating under the surface of the water, his eyes open.*

RITA *goes slowly into the house.*

Time passes: night into dawn. ALFRED, *dressed as the day before but wearing a hat, comes up the steps from the beach and sits. He throws his hat onto the table and leans on his arms, gazing over the fjord.*

A heavy mist develops, almost masking the fjord. It's the next afternoon.

ASTA *comes from the house, carrying her parasol and her bag. She goes to him cautiously.*

ASTA. You shouldn't be out in this weather, Alfred.

ALFRED *nods slowly.*

Have you been here long?

Silence.

ALFRED. It can't be true.

ASTA. Freddie...

ASTA *lays her hand gently on his arm. He stares at her.*

ALFRED. Wouldn't it be wonderful to wake up and find I'd been dreaming?

ASTA. I wish I could make that happen.

He looks out at the fjord.

ALFRED. The water looks so flat... so thick... so leaden... just a flash of yellow... and the clouds flickering on the surface...

ASTA. Don't, Freddie...

ALFRED....but underneath, in the deep, there's the undertow...

ASTA. Don't, Freddie...

ALFRED. I suppose you imagine his body's nearby, don't you, Asta? It isn't. The current sweeps everything straight out to sea.

She buries her face in her hands.

ASTA. Oh God... oh God...

ALFRED. Eyolf's a long way away from us now.

ASTA. Don't, Freddie...

ALFRED. You're clever, you can work it out for yourself: it's been twenty-eight hours, no, twenty-nine, so it'll –

ASTA. *Freddie!*

She screams, covering her ears as she does so. He grips the table.

ALFRED. What do you think it means?

ASTA. What?

ALFRED. What's happened.

ASTA. Means?

ALFRED. Yes, what d'you think it *means*. It has to have a *meaning* – life, fate, whatever you call it – it can't be so completely meaningless.

ASTA. How can we know?

ALFRED (*parroting her*). *How can we know*? Maybe it's all random. Maybe we're just drifting wrecks. That's what it seems like.

ASTA. It only seems?

ALFRED (*violently*). Well, maybe you've got a better explanation? I don't. Eyolf was just on the edge of a life of rich, of... *infinite* possibilities. He would've filled my life with pride and with happiness and then some crazy bitch has to appear with a mongrel in a sack and –

ASTA. We don't know how it happened.

ALFRED. We do. Those boys saw her row out over the fjord and Eyolf standing at the end of the jetty and they saw him staring at her and then he got dizzy and... and... and then he fell into the water and... and... and... (*Stops.*) disappeared.

ASTA. But there's –

ALFRED. There's no doubt about it, she dragged him down into the water.

ASTA. But why?

ALFRED. Why? Exactly, why should she? It can't have been revenge. Eyolf never did her any harm, he didn't call her names, he didn't throw stones at her dog, he'd never ever seen her or her dog till yesterday, so the whole thing is completely senseless... meaningless. And yet fate demands it.

ASTA. Have you said this to Rita?

ALFRED. It's easier to talk to you about it... and about everything else.

ASTA sits at the table, then takes sewing materials and a small paper parcel out of her bag. She undoes the parcel.

What's that?

ASTA. Black crêpe.

ALFRED. What for?

ASTA. Rita asked me to do it. Shall I?

ALFRED. Why not?

She picks up the hat and starts to sew the crêpe onto it.

Where's Rita?

ASTA. Walking. With Bjarne.

ALFRED. Is he here?

ASTA. He came out by the midday train.

ALFRED. I'm surprised.

ASTA. He was fond of Eyolf.

ALFRED. And he's loyal.

ASTA. Yes, he's that.

ALFRED. You're really keen on him…

ASTA. Yes, I am.

ALFRED.…and yet you can't make up your mind –

ASTA. Don't, Freddie –

ALFRED. Why can't you?

ASTA. Don't ask me, please.

She holds out his hat to him, the crêpe band around it.

Your hat's done.

ALFRED. Thank you.

ASTA. Now for the arm.

ALFRED. Do I have to have crêpe on that too?

ASTA. The left one.

ALFRED. If you must.

She moves her chair close to him and begins to sew a band on his jacket.

ASTA. You have to keep your arm still or I'll prick you.

ALFRED. This is like old times.

ASTA. It is, isn't it?

ALFRED. You started mending my clothes when you were quite little.

ASTA. I wasn't very good at it.

ALFRED. Actually, sewing black crêpe on my cap was the first sewing you ever did.

ASTA. Was it?

ALFRED. When Papa died.

ASTA. Could I sew then?

ALFRED. You were very young.

ASTA. I was tiny.

ALFRED. Then two years later when your mother died you sewed a crêpe band on my sleeve.

ASTA. I thought it was the right thing to do.

ALFRED. It was the right thing to do, Asta. There was just the two of us then.

She puts her sewing materials back in the bag.

Have you finished?

ASTA. Yes. It was a lovely time, Freddie.

ALFRED. Yes, it was. Hard work though.

ASTA. For you.

ALFRED. You worked hard too. Dear... old... Eyolf.

ASTA. Don't start that stupid stuff again.

ALFRED. Well, you'd have been called Eyolf if you'd been a boy.

ASTA. If. How could you have been so childish?

ALFRED. Was I childish?

ASTA. You were at university and you were ashamed of being an orphan and only having me for family.

ALFRED. *You* were ashamed.

ASTA. No, I just felt sorry for you.

ALFRED. You got out my old clothes.

ASTA. Do you remember the blue shirt and the shorts?

He smiles as he looks at her.

ALFRED. I remember how you looked when you put them on.

ASTA. It was only when we were alone.

ALFRED. We were very serious and very pleased with ourselves. And I always called you... (*Wryly.*) Eyolf.

ASTA. I hope you've never told Rita about this.

ALFRED. I did tell her once.

ASTA. Why?

ALFRED. Well, you're supposed to tell your wife everything. Well, nearly everything.

ASTA. I suppose you are.

ALFRED. Eyolf...

ASTA. Freddie...

He takes her hand and there's a moment's silence and then suddenly he jumps up.

ALFRED. Oh God, how can I sit here and —

ASTA. What's the matter?

ALFRED. I'd forgotten him. Completely. I'd wiped him out of my mind.

ASTA. He was still there.

ALFRED. No, he wasn't, I didn't think of him for a moment while we were talking, I completely forgot him.

ASTA. Surely you've got to rest from grieving.

ALFRED. No, I won't, I mustn't, I shouldn't stop grieving. I can't anyway, I've got to be with him.

He goes towards the steps. ASTA *follows him and holds him back.*

ASTA. Don't go to the fjord.

ALFRED. I have to go to him, I have to take the boat.

She grabs hold of him, terrified.

Let me go, Asta.

ASTA. DON'T GO!!!

She grabs hold of ALFRED, *who gives in to her. She takes his arm and leads him towards the chaise.*

ALFRED. All right, I won't, just leave me alone.

ASTA. You've got to stop brooding, Freddie.

ALFRED. All right, *all right*!

He breaks away from her and goes to sit by the table. She takes his arm.

ASTA. Not there.

ALFRED. Leave me alone.

ASTA. I won't, you'll only sit there staring.

She drags him to the chaise, forces him to sit down and sits next to him.

You can talk to me.

ALFRED. It was good not to think for a moment.

ASTA. You have to do that, Freddie.

ALFRED. But don't you think it's terrible that I can do that?

ASTA. You can't keep on and on thinking the same thing.

ALFRED. You're right. I've been sitting here, torturing myself with these... agonising thoughts and...

ASTA. Yes?

ALFRED. And d'you know what, Asta? (*Half-laugh.*) Huh...

ASTA. What?

ALFRED. In the middle of all that... agony, I found myself wondering what we were going have for dinner.

ASTA. But that's fine –

ALFRED. Fine, yes, fine.

He takes her hand.

I'm so glad you're here.

ASTA. You've got Rita.

ALFRED. She's not family, it isn't the same as having a sister.

ASTA. Is that what you really think?

ALFRED. Of course. Our family is special. Don't you remember what we used to say: that all our names start with a vowel, all our relatives are poor and we all have the same colour eyes.

ASTA. *I* don't.

ALFRED. No, you're not remotely like the rest of us, you take after your mother, but all the same...

ASTA. What?

ALFRED....living together's made us like each other, I mean in the way we think.

ASTA. I've just modelled myself on you. I owe you everything, well, everything that's been good in my life.

ALFRED. You don't owe me anything, Asta.

ASTA. I *do*, you've sacrificed –

ALFRED. I haven't sacrificed anything, all I've done is love you ever since you were a little girl and I've always thought that there was so much that I had to make up for.

ASTA. What?

ALFRED. Not on my account, but...

ASTA. But what?

ALFRED. On our father's.

ASTA *half-rises from the chaise, then sits down again.*

ASTA. What do you mean?

ALFRED. He was horrible to you.

ASTA. Don't *say* that.

ALFRED. It's true, he didn't love you the way he should have...

ASTA....maybe not the way he loved you...

ALFRED....and he was cruel to your mother – in the last years anyway.

ASTA *is fighting tears.*

ASTA. Mama was much younger than him.

ALFRED. You mean they weren't suited?

ASTA. Maybe.

ALFRED. He was fine with everyone else.

ASTA. She didn't always behave well.

ALFRED. You mean towards Papa?

ASTA. Yes.

ALFRED. I never saw that.

She stands, struggling with tears.

ASTA. Oh, Freddie, let's let the dead rest.

She goes towards the edge of the veranda. He follows.

ALFRED. They won't let *us* rest, Asta.

ASTA. It'll get easier with time.

ALFRED. Will it? How do I live until it does?

Imploringly, laying her hands on his shoulders.

ASTA. Talk to Rita, please…

ALFRED. Don't ask me to do that, I can't!

He breaks away from her angrily, then he takes her hand and holds it, hard.

Let me stay with you.

ASTA. I won't leave you.

ALFRED. Thank you… Where's my little Eyolf now?

ASTA. Oh, Freddie, don't.

ALFRED. I mean the little one not the big, clever one. Can she tell me? Of course not. He's gone.

ASTA. They're coming.

She looks towards the stairs, taking her hand from ALFRED*'s.*

RITA *and* BORGHEIM *come up the steps of the veranda, she leading the way. She wears a dark dress and a black veil over her head. He has an umbrella under his arm.* ALFRED *goes towards her but she walks past him.*

ALFRED. How are you, Rita?

RITA. What do *you* think?

She lifts her veil and takes her hat off, putting it on the table.

I've been looking for you.

ALFRED. Down there?

RITA. What've you been doing?

ALFRED. Talking to Asta.

RITA. Yes, but before that? You've been avoiding me all morning.

ALFRED. I've been sitting here looking out over the fjord.

RITA. Euuch, how can you?

ALFRED. I prefer to be by myself.

RITA. And sit like a statue.

ALFRED. I don't want to move.

RITA *paces restlessly.*

RITA. I can't bear to be here, looking at the fjord.

ALFRED. It's *because* the fjord is –

RITA (*to* BORGHEIM). Don't you think he should stop staring?

BORGHEIM (*to* ALFRED). It might be better for you.

ALFRED. I want to stay where I am.

RITA. Then I'll stay with you.

ALFRED. All right. Do. You too, Asta.

ASTA (*whispering to* BORGHEIM). Let's leave them alone.

BORGHEIM (*to* ASTA). Shall we go down the beach for the very very last time?

ASTA. Let's.

ASTA picks up her parasol and she and BORGHEIM *go down the steps.* ALFRED *wanders aimlessly then sits at the table, looking down.* RITA *comes and stands facing him.*

RITA. Can you believe that we've lost Eyolf?

ALFRED. We have to believe it.

RITA. I can't... *I* can't... and I'm going to be haunted for the rest of my life by that sight.

ALFRED. What sight?

RITA. Oh, I haven't seen it, they just described it.

ALFRED. What?

RITA. I got Borgheim to go down with me to the jetty...

ALFRED. Why?

RITA. ...to ask the boys how it happened.

ALFRED. But we know already.

RITA. I wanted to know more.

ALFRED. And?

RITA. And it's not true that he disappeared immediately.

ALFRED. Is that what they say now?

RITA. They say they saw him in the clear water lying on the bottom.

ALFRED. And they didn't move to save him.

RITA. I don't suppose they could.

ALFRED. They could all swim.

RITA. They said he was lying on his back, with his eyes open.

ALFRED. But not moving?

RITA. And then something came and carried him out to sea. The undertow.

ALFRED. And that was the last they saw of him.

RITA. Yes.

ALFRED. And we'll never... never, ever... ever see him again.

   RITA *is suffocating with tears. She keens in agony.*

RITA. I'll always see him lying down there.

ALFRED. With his eyes open.

RITA. Yes, with his eyes wide open. I can see them, I can see them now.

ALFRED *stands and looks at* RITA *with quiet menace*.

ALFRED. Were they evil, those eyes, Rita?

RITA. Evil...?

He moves closer to her, speaking right in her face.

ALFRED. Yes, evil. Were the eyes that stared up from the seabed evil?

RITA. What...?

ALFRED. *WERE THE CHILD'S EYES EVIL?*

RITA. *STOP IT!*

He turns away from her.

ALFRED. You've got what you wanted.

RITA. What did I want?

ALFRED. You wanted to get rid of Eyolf.

RITA. I've never wanted that, all I wanted was that Eyolf wouldn't come between the two of us.

ALFRED. Well, he doesn't come between us any more.

RITA. Or maybe more than ever, oh, that awful sight...

ALFRED. The evil eyes of a child.

RITA. You're frightening me, I've never seen you like this.

ALFRED. Grief makes you cruel.

RITA. I know.

ALFRED *looks out over the fjord.* RITA *sits at the table.*

A silence. Then he turns back to her.

ALFRED. You never loved him. Ever.

RITA. Eyolf would never let me love him.

ALFRED. You didn't want to.

RITA. I did, I did want to, there was somebody in my way.

ALFRED. Do you mean me?

RITA. No, not at first.

ALFRED. Then who?

RITA. His aunt.

ALFRED. Asta?

RITA. Yes. Asta stood in my way.

ALFRED. How can you say that?

RITA. She took him over from the moment that... that the accident happened.

ALFRED. If she did, she did it out of love.

RITA. I don't want to share love!

ALFRED. We should have shared our love for him.

RITA. We? You never really loved him either.

ALFRED. Me?

RITA. Yes, you. You were too much in love with your book. *Human Responsibility*. Hah...

ALFRED. I sacrificed my book for Eyolf.

RITA. Not because you loved him.

ALFRED. Then why, do you think?

RITA. Because you were consumed with self-doubt, because you'd lost your confidence, because you'd begun to wonder whether you had any talent at all.

ALFRED. Oh, is that what you think?

RITA. And then you needed something new to occupy you and I wasn't enough for you any more.

ALFRED. Things change, you know that.

RITA. That's why you wanted to make poor Eyolf into a child prodigy,

ALFRED. I wanted to make him a happy person, that's all.

RITA. But you didn't do it out of love for him. Look at yourself. Be honest, don't lie to yourself.

ALFRED. And you're honest?

RITA. As much as you are.

ALFRED. If it's true what you're saying then Eyolf wasn't ever really our child.

RITA. No. We never loved him

ALFRED. And yet we're in agonies of grief over him.

RITA. Yes it's odd, isn't it, that we should grieve like this over someone we hardly knew?

ALFRED. Don't say that.

RITA. We never won his love, either of us.

There's a moment of stillness, then ALFRED *turns on* RITA *violently.*

ALFRED. It's all your fault!

RITA. Me?

ALFRED. It was your fault that he became what he became, it was your fault that he couldn't save himself when he fell into the water –

RITA. Don't you dare blame me –

ALFRED. It was you that left the baby on the table –

RITA. He was asleep on a mattress and you'd said you'd look after him.

ALFRED. But you had to come, didn't you, you had to come, you had to take your clothes off –

RITA. Oh, just admit that you forgot the baby –

ALFRED. *YES I FORGOT THE BABY, WE WERE MAKING LOVE!*

RITA. This is unbearable –

ALFRED. And that's when you condemned Eyolf to death.

RITA. You were there too.

ALFRED. Oh yes I'm to blame too, we both are, we've *sinned*, both of us, if that's how you want to look at it, and Eyolf's death was our retribution.

RITA. Retribution?

ALFRED. A judgement. What we deserved. When he was alive, after the accident, we couldn't bear to look at his... withered leg and his stick and his pain and what we have now – all our heartache and our grief and our... our... *misery* – is just our conscience gnawing at us, Rita, nothing else.

RITA. This is hopeless, we'll make each other insane.

They're both exhausted by the argument and slump like spent swimmers.

ALFRED. I had a dream about Eyolf last night. I thought I saw him coming up from the jetty, running just like the other boys. He was alive, and he wasn't crippled. And I thought 'this... torture was just a dream' and oh how I thanked and blessed –

He stops himself.

RITA. Who?

ALFRED. Who?

RITA. Who did you thank and bless?

ALFRED. It was a dream.

RITA. Was it the God you don't believe in?

ALFRED. I was asleep.

RITA. You shouldn't have taken my faith away.

ALFRED. Would it have been better to let you go through life believing in fairytales?

RITA. It would have been better for me because I'd have had something to comfort me, now I'm completely at sea. I'm lost.

ALFRED. If you could choose... if you could, if you could follow Eyolf to whatever, wherever he is...?

RITA. What?

ALFRED. If you could be sure that you'd find him again, get to know him, get to understand him...?

RITA. What? *What?*

ALFRED. Would you... voluntarily... take the leap over to him? Willingly leave everything behind? Give up your life for, I don't know... heaven? Would you, Rita?

RITA. You mean now?

ALFRED. Yes. Now. Would you?

RITA. I don't know. No, I think I'd choose to stay here with you.

ALFRED. For my sake?

RITA. For your sake.

ALFRED. And later? Then what?

A silence.

RITA. I couldn't leave you.

ALFRED. What if I joined Eyolf and you were certain that you'd meet both of us there?

RITA. I'd want to... so much, but...

ALFRED. But what?

RITA. I couldn't, I couldn't, not even for... oh, for the joys of heaven.

ALFRED. I couldn't either.

RITA. No you couldn't, could you?

ALFRED. We belong here. On earth. Being alive.

RITA. Yes, we can be happy here.

ALFRED. Happy? Huh.

RITA. What if...?

ALFRED. What?

RITA. Could we... would it be possible... could... can we ever forget him?

ALFRED. Forget Eyolf?

RITA. Forget ourselves, forget the guilt.

ALFRED. Is that what you want?

RITA. If it were possible. *I can't bear this!*

She stands suddenly, shouting as she does so.

Can't we do something to make us forget?

ALFRED. What?

RITA. We could travel.

ALFRED. You don't like travelling.

RITA. Well, let's have hordes of people here, anything to anaesthetise us.

ALFRED. I couldn't live like that, I need to work again.

RITA. To *work*? Do you mean on that book that's been like a brick wall between us.

ALFRED. There'll always be a wall between us.

RITA. Why?

ALFRED. Because his eyes'll always be watching us.

RITA. Don't...

ALFRED. Rita, our love's been like a bonfire and it's burnt itself out.

RITA. Burnt out?

ALFRED. Yes, burnt out.

She stops moving and stands, turned to stone.

RITA. How dare you say that.

ALFRED. It's dead, Rita, but I can see the possibility of a sort of... of a sort of... resurrection.

RITA. I don't give a damn about resurrection.

ALFRED. Rita...

RITA. I don't go flapping about with fishes' blood in my veins, I'm a hot-blooded human being and I won't be shut up for life in a prison of guilt with someone who doesn't even *belong* to me!

ALFRED. It had to end some time, Rita.

RITA. Had to? We had a love that wrapped us in flames.

ALFRED. I wasn't wrapped in flames.

RITA. What did you feel for me then?

ALFRED. Fear.

RITA. Oh of course you did, then how did I manage to win you?

ALFRED. You were entrancingly beautiful, Rita, you capsized me.

RITA. Was that the only reason? Tell me: was *that* the only reason?

ALFRED. No.

RITA. I can guess what it was, it was my 'burnished gold and great green forests', wasn't it?

A silence.

Wasn't it?

ALFRED. Yes.

RITA. How could you, how could you *do* that?

ALFRED. I had Asta to think of.

RITA. *Asta.* So it was *Asta* that brought us together?

ALFRED. She didn't know anything about it, she doesn't know now.

RITA. It was *Asta*, just the same, oh no, it was Eyolf, your little Eyolf, wasn't it?

ALFRED. Eyolf?

RITA. Yes, you used to call her Eyolf, didn't you, you told me, don't you remember?

She comes up to him, almost whispers in his ear.

It was at that entrancingly beautiful moment, wasn't it, when you were capsized by *la petite mort*.

ALFRED. I don't remember.

RITA. Don't you? When 'our' little Eyolf almost died? Almost another *petite mort*.

ALFRED. That's the retribution.

RITA. Yes, that's the retribution.

ASTA *and* BORGHEIM *climb the steps to the veranda. She's carrying some water lilies.*

Well, Asta, have you and Mr Borgheim talked things over?

ASTA. Oh, pretty much.

ASTA *puts down her parasol and lays the flowers upon a chair.*

BORGHEIM. Miss Allmers has been very quiet during our walk.

RITA. Oh, has she? Well, Alfred and I have talked things over more than thoroughly…

ASTA. What did you…

RITA.…in fact, enough to last a lifetime, I'd say.

RITA *picks up her hat from the table and goes towards the house.*

Let's go in. We're going to have lots of guests from now on, Alfred and I can't live alone.

ALFRED. I have to have a word with Asta.

RITA. Oh, of course. Well then, follow me, Mr Borgheim.

RITA *and* BORGHEIM *go into the house.*

ASTA. What's happening, Freddie?

ALFRED. I can't stand it any longer.

ASTA. With Rita you mean?

ALFRED. We can't go on living together.

She grabs his arm, shaking him.

ASTA. Don't say things like that.

ALFRED. It's the truth, I'm telling you, we're making each other vile and cruel.

ASTA. What do you want to do?

ALFRED. Get away from everything.

ASTA. Be alone?

ALFRED. The way it used to be, yes.

ASTA. You can't live alone.

ALFRED. I did before.

ASTA. You had me with you then.

ALFRED *tries to take her hand, but* ASTA *avoids it.*

ALFRED. I want that again.

ASTA. You can't.

ALFRED. Is it Bjarne?

ASTA. No, no it isn't.

ALFRED. Then I can come home to you, I *must*, I need to wash this life away, I need to be clean –

ASTA. Freddie, you can't treat Rita like this.

ALFRED. I know, I *know*, but think of it, Asta, think how we could live together, how we used to live together, wasn't it one long holiday?

ASTA. We can't repeat it.

ALFRED. You mean I've been ruined by marriage?

ASTA. No I don't mean that.

ALFRED. Well then, we can live our old life.

ASTA. We can't, Freddie.

ALFRED. We *can*, the love between a brother and sister is –

ASTA. Is what?

ALFRED. Is the only relationship that doesn't change.

ASTA. But if our relationship wasn't...?

ALFRED. Wasn't what?

ASTA. Wasn't that.

ALFRED. What d'you mean?

ASTA. The letters I told you about, the letters to Mama...

ALFRED. Yes...?

ASTA. You have to read them...

ALFRED. Why?

ASTA. Because you'll see...

ALFRED. What?

ASTA. That I'm not, that I have no right, oh, that I have no right to your father's name.

She goes to her bag, gets the letters out.

ALFRED. What are you talking about?

ASTA. Read the letters, then you'll see and maybe you'll be able to forgive Mama.

ALFRED. I can't get my head round this... I can't... I can't, you're saying –

ASTA. I'm saying I'm not your sister, Freddie.

A silence.

ALFRED. Well, how does that change anything?

ASTA. It changes everything, we're not brother and sister.

ALFRED. But it's no less precious.

ASTA. Everything changes. It's a law, that's what you always say.

ALFRED. You mean –

ASTA. Don't say anything, Freddie, please…

She picks the flowers from the chair.

You see these water lilies?

ALFRED. They have their roots deep in the river.

ASTA. They're from where it flows into the fjord. (*Holding out the flowers.*) For you.

ALFRED. Thank you.

ASTA. From Eyolf.

ALFRED. Which one?

ASTA. Both.

She picks up her parasol.

Come with me to Rita.

She goes into the house. ALFRED *picks up his hat from the table and stands motionless, facing away from the fjord.*

The view of the fjord fades into water and EYOLF's *body can be seen floating under the surface, his eyes open. His eyes become closer and closer until they fill the cyclorama.* ALFRED *whispers as he follows* ASTA *into the house.*

ALFRED. Asta… Eyolf… little Asta… little Eyolf…

BORGHEIM *comes up the steps from the garden. He carries a travelling bag. He waits, restlessly, looking out over the fjord.*

The eyes fade to the image of fjord. A clear sky, late sunset, on the blink of twilight.

ASTA *comes out of the house. She's wearing a hat, has her parasol and her bag on a strap over her shoulder.*

ASTA. You've been waiting for me?

BORGHEIM. I wanted to say goodbye, I hope not for ever.

ASTA. You're persistent.

BORGHEIM. You have to be to build roads.

ASTA. Have you seen Alfred?

BORGHEIM. I saw them both earlier.

ASTA. Together?

BORGHEIM. Separately. Don't you think it's a bit heartless to leave them?

ASTA. I have to.

BORGHEIM. Well, if you must, then you must.

ASTA. You're going too, aren't you?

BORGHEIM. By the train. Are you?

ASTA. The ferry.

BORGHEIM. So we're going our separate ways.

ASTA. Yes.

A silence.

BORGHEIM. I'm so upset about Eyolf...

ASTA. I know...

BORGHEIM....I feel, such, I don't know... pain, I've never felt like this.

ASTA. It'll go away.

BORGHEIM. Will it?

ASTA. Like a summer shower, once you're away from here...

BORGHEIM. I'd have to be a long way away...

ASTA....and you've got your new road to think about.

BORGHEIM. But no one to help me with it.

ASTA. Oh, come on...

BORGHEIM. No one to share the thrill of it. I want to *share* the excitement.

ASTA. Not the trouble and strife?

BORGHEIM. You can always get through that stuff on your own.

ASTA. But you have to share the excitement?

BORGHEIM. What's the point of being happy if you can't share it?

ASTA. Perhaps.

BORGHEIM. It might do in the short run but it takes two to be happy.

ASTA. Not more?

BORGHEIM. Well, that's different. Are you sure you don't want to share happiness, even success with someone who needs you and... and of course the 'trouble and strife'?

ASTA. I've tried it.

BORGHEIM. Have you?

ASTA. Yes, all the time that Freddie – Alfred – that my brother and I lived together.

BORGHEIM. Oh, of course, your brother. That's not the same thing, that's... um... harmony not happiness.

ASTA. Wonderful, all the same.

BORGHEIM. But imagine what it'd have been like if he hadn't been your brother?

ASTA. Then we'd never have lived together. Anyway, I was a child and he wasn't much older.

She starts to stand, but sits again. There's a slightly awkward silence.

BORGHEIM. Was it really so wonderful, that time?

ASTA. Yes. Yes, it was.

BORGHEIM. What was so wonderful about it?

ASTA. There was so much.

BORGHEIM. What?

ASTA. Just things...

BORGHEIM. Such as...?

ASTA. Oh, such as the time when Freddie had got his scholarship, or when he got a job as a teacher, or when he'd work at home on an article and he'd read it to me and then it'd appear in a magazine and... oh, just trivial things.

BORGHEIM. I can't understand how he could have given up such a wonderful life.

ASTA. He got married.

BORGHEIM. Did you find that difficult?

ASTA. At first. I thought I'd lost him.

BORGHEIM. But you hadn't.

ASTA. No.

BORGHEIM. But how could he, I mean what do you think made him get married when he could have gone on living with you?

ASTA. The law of change, I suppose.

BORGHEIM. The law of change?

ASTA. Change is subject to a law, he says. It's like gravity.

BORGHEIM. Oh rubbish, I don't believe that for a moment.

ASTA *stands*.

ASTA. Maybe you'll believe in it someday.

BORGHEIM. Never. Asta, listen, please be sensible for once, please –

ASTA. Don't start that again –

BORGHEIM. I can't give you up. Your brother had everything he wanted, he was perfectly happy without you, he didn't need you, and now... this thing happens –

ASTA. What do you mean?

BORGHEIM. Eyolf, what else?

ASTA. Oh, yes...

BORGHEIM. What more is there for you to do here? You don't have that boy to take care of, you don't have any obligations –

ASTA. Oh, please, don't make it so difficult for me.

BORGHEIM. I have to, I'd be mad not to, I may not see you again for months, years. Anything might happen before we meet again.

ASTA. Oh, so you do believe in the law of change.

BORGHEIM. No, of course not, anyway, there's nothing to change. In you at least. I mean, I can see you don't really care for me.

ASTA. I do.

BORGHEIM. Not enough, not the way that I want you to. God, Asta, can't you see how wrong you are? There could be a lifetime of happiness waiting and you're just letting it pass you by. Don't you think you'll come to regret it?

ASTA. I don't know, I only know all this... bright future isn't for me.

BORGHEIM. So I'll have to work alone?

ASTA. I do wish I could be with you to share the bad times as well as the happy ones but...

BORGHEIM. Would you if you could?

ASTA. Yes, I would.

BORGHEIM. But you can't?

ASTA. Would you be happy with only half of me?

BORGHEIM. No. You'd have to be entirely mine.

ASTA. Then I can't.

BORGHEIM. Goodbye then, Asta.

He turns and goes towards the steps. As he does so, ALFRED *comes up the steps.* BORGHEIM *stops when he sees him.*

ALFRED. Has Rita been out here?

BORGHEIM. No, no one but Asta.

ALFRED *moves towards* ASTA.

ASTA. Shall I go into the house and look for her?

ALFRED. No, it doesn't matter.

ALFRED. Are you going?

BORGHEIM. Yes, I really am going.

ALFRED (*glancing at* ASTA). You've made sure you've got a good travelling companion.

BORGHEIM. I'm going alone.

ALFRED. Alone?

BORGHEIM. Alone.

ALFRED. Really?

BORGHEIM. Really. And I'll stay alone.

ALFRED. There's something awful about being alone, it turns my blood to ice...

ASTA. You're not alone.

ALFRED. There might also be something awful about *that*...

ASTA. Don't, Freddie.

ALFRED....but if you're not going with him, why don't you stay here with us?

ASTA. I can't, I have to go to town now.

ALFRED. But only to town. Are you listening to me, Asta?

ASTA. Yes.

ALFRED. Promise me that you'll come again soon.

ASTA. I can't promise that.

ALFRED. We'll meet in town then.

ASTA. You have to stay here for now.

ALFRED *ignores her and turns to* BORGHEIM.

ALFRED. I think you're lucky to be going alone.

BORGHEIM. How can you say that?

ALFRED. You don't know who you might meet later, on the journey.

ASTA. Freddie...

ALFRED. You might meet the right travelling companion when it's too late.

ASTA. Oh, Freddie, don't...

BORGHEIM *looks between the two of them.*

BORGHEIM. What the hell's going on?

RITA *comes from the house carrying a lamp. She's wearing her white dressing gown, her hair is wild-looking. It's twilight now. She puts the lamp on the table but doesn't light it.*

RITA. You're all deserting me.

ASTA. You said you wanted to be alone.

RITA. Yes, but I can't. It's getting too dark. I seem to see big eyes staring at me.

ASTA. You shouldn't be afraid of those eyes.

RITA. How can you say that?

ALFRED. Asta, I'm begging you, please, for God's sake, stay here with Rita.

RITA. Please do, Asta, please...

ASTA. I want to so much –

RITA. Do it then, please, Asta, we can't face the grief alone.

ALFRED. Why don't you say the guilt?

RITA. Whatever you call it, we can't bear it alone. I'm begging you, Asta, stay here and help us, take Eyolf's place –

ASTA. Eyolf's?

RITA (*to* ALFRED). You want it, don't you?

ALFRED. If she does.

RITA. You used to call her your Eyolf.

RITA *takes* ASTA*'s hand.*

You'll be our little Eyolf, Asta, like you were before.

ALFRED. Stay with us, Asta. With Rita. With me. With your *brother*.

ASTA *snatches her hand from* RITA.

ASTA. Bjarne, what time does the ferry leave?

BORGHEIM. Soon. Now.

ASTA. I have to catch it. Do you want to come with me?

BORGHEIM. Come with you? Yes, yes, I do.

ASTA. Let's go, then.

RITA. Oh, so that's the way it is. Well, then, of course you can't stay with us.

ASTA. Thanks for everything, Rita.

ASTA *throws her arms round* RITA*'s neck. Then she goes to* ALFRED *and takes his hand between both of hers.*

Goodbye, Freddie, goodbye, goodbye, goodbye, goodbye, goodbye, good–

ALFRED. It looks like you're running away.

ASTA. Yes, I'm running away.

ALFRED. From me.

ASTA (*whispering*). And from me.

ALFRED *shies back as if he'd been slapped as* ASTA *rushes down the steps at the back.* BORGHEIM *waves to* RITA *and* ALFRED*, and follows her.*

RITA *leans against the door to the house.* ALFRED *goes to the edge of the veranda and stands there staring towards the fjord.*

The noise of the ferry chugging across the fjord.

ALFRED. There's the ferry.

RITA. I don't dare look at it.

ALFRED. You don't dare?

RITA. It has glowing eyes: a red one and a green one.

ALFRED. Those are just its navigation lights.

RITA. They're its eyes. They stare out of the dark. And into my darkness.

ALFRED. It's putting in to shore.

RITA. Where?

ALFRED. At the jetty, of course.

RITA. How can it go there?

ALFRED. It has to.

RITA. Where Eyolf drowned, how can it go there?

ALFRED. Life's pitiless, Rita.

RITA. People are heartless, they don't care for the living or for the dead.

ALFRED. You're right, life goes on as if nothing had happened.

RITA. Nothing has happened, only to us.

ALFRED. And all that pain you endured giving birth to him was pointless. He's vanished without a trace.

RITA. I can't bear the thought that he's gone.

He turns to her.

ALFRED. You managed well enough without him when he was alive. You'd often spend half the day without seeing him.

RITA. But I knew that I could see him whenever I wanted to.

ALFRED. Well, that's why we wasted the little time we had with him.

The deep sound of the ferry's bell can be heard, announcing the departure. ALFRED *goes to the edge of the veranda.*

RITA. The bell's ringing again.

ALFRED. Yes. The ferry's leaving.

RITA. I don't mean that bell, I mean the bell I've heard ringing in my ears all day.

ALFRED. What bell?

RITA. I hear it so clearly. Like a funeral bell. And always with the same words.

ALFRED. What words?

RITA. Your – boy – is – drowned – your – boy – is – drowned. Surely you can hear it?

ALFRED. I can't hear anything. There's nothing to hear.

RITA. I can hear it clearly.

ALFRED. They're on the ferry, Rita. On the way to town.

RITA. Can you really not hear it? Your – boy – is – drowned – your – boy – is – drowned.

ALFRED *goes to* RITA *as she moves towards the sound of the bell.*

ALFRED. The bells are telling us that Asta and Borgheim are gone. That Asta is gone.

RITA. Then I suppose you'll be going soon.

ALFRED. What do you mean by that?

RITA. I mean you'll follow your sister.

ALFRED. Has she said something?

RITA. You said it: we came together or whatever you call it, got *married*, for Asta's sake.

ALFRED. But it's you who hold me here.

RITA. Do I? Am I still 'entrancingly beautiful' to you?

ALFRED. Well, perhaps the law of change will keep us together.

The bells stop.

It's dark now. Only the stars and a light from the house, slicing across the veranda. RITA *goes to the table and slowly lights the lamp.*

RITA. 'The law of change...' *I'm* changing. I am, it's very painful.

ALFRED. Painful?

RITA. Like a birth.

ALFRED. Perhaps it's a resurrection.

RITA. I'm losing all my happiness.

ALFRED. That's not loss, that's *gain*.

RITA. Oh, what rubbish, good God, we're human beings, we're *flesh and blood*!

ALFRED. We're part of nature too.

RITA. Maybe you are, I'm not.

ALFRED. Yes you are, more than you think.

She's finished lighting the lamp and comes towards him.

RITA. Why don't you start your work again?

ALFRED. You hate it.

RITA. I'm easier to please now, I'm willing to share you with your book.

ALFRED. Why?

RITA. To keep you here with me, to have you near me.

ALFRED. I can't be of much help to you, Rita.

RITA. Perhaps I could help you.

ALFRED. With my book?

RITA. To live your life.

ALFRED. I seem to have no life to live.

RITA. Well then, to endure your life.

He turns away from her, speaking almost to himself.

ALFRED. I think it would be best for both of us if we lived apart.

RITA. Where would you go? To Asta?

ALFRED. No, not to Asta.

RITA. Then where?

ALFRED. Solitude.

RITA. Do you mean the mountains?

ALFRED. Yes.

RITA. Oh, that's just a fantasy, you couldn't live there.

ALFRED. I'm drawn to them.

RITA. Why? Why? Just tell me why?

ALFRED. I'll tell you if you sit down.

RITA. Something that happened to you there?

ALFRED. Yes.

RITA. Something that you kept from us? You shouldn't be so secretive about everything.

ALFRED. I'll tell you if you sit down.

RITA. All right, tell me.

She sits on the chaise. ALFRED *remains standing.*

ALFRED. I was walking high in the mountains and I came to a desolate... to a wide volcanic lake. I had to cross the lake but I was alone and there was no boat.

RITA. And?

ALFRED. Without looking at my map I went into a valley at the side of the lake where I thought that there'd be a pass through the mountains which would come down on the other side.

RITA. And you got lost.

ALFRED. There weren't any paths or tracks and I walked all day and all the next night and I thought I'd never see the face of a human being again.

RITA. Were you thinking of us?

ALFRED. No, it was strange, you and Eyolf seemed to have drifted a long, long way away from me. Asta, too.

RITA. What *did* you think of?

ALFRED. I didn't think. I was dragging myself along the edge of a precipice and wallowing in the peace and the... luxury of death.

RITA. Don't –

ALFRED. I wasn't afraid of anything. Death and I were like two good travelling companions. It all seemed so natural, so ordinary. We don't live to be old in my family and –

RITA. Don't say things like that, you came out of it alive.

ALFRED. I suddenly found I was where I wanted to be, on the other side of the lake and –

RITA. You must have been terrified that night but you won't admit it, will you?

ALFRED. I came to a decision. That was why I came straight home to Eyolf.

RITA. Too late.

ALFRED *sits on the chaise next to* RITA.

ALFRED. Yes and then my... travelling companion came and... took him away and then I realised the foulness of death, the horror of it. And of life too but we don't dare to tear ourselves away from it so we're stuck on this earth. Both of us.

RITA. We are, aren't we?

She leans against him. The two of them sit together like an old couple, too tired to protest.

Let's live our life together as long as we can.

ALFRED. Live our life? We have nothing to live for. Wherever I look there's nothing.

RITA. You'll leave me, won't you, sooner or later?

ALFRED. Leave with my 'travelling companion'?

RITA. I mean you'll leave me because you think it's only here, with me, that you have nothing to live for. Isn't that right? Isn't that what you're thinking?

ALFRED. What if it were?

Suddenly shouts and the noise of angry voices and screams are heard from down below.

RITA. What's that?

ALFRED *goes to the edge of the veranda.* RITA *jumps up.*

They've found him! They've found him!

ALFRED. He'll never be found.

RITA. Then what's happening?

ALFRED. Just the usual brawling.

RITA. On the beach?

ALFRED. That whole damn village ought to be wiped out. The men are always drunk when they come home from work and they beat their children and their wives scream –

RITA. Shouldn't we get someone to help?

ALFRED. Help *them*? They didn't help Eyolf, let them suffer the way he did, the scum.

RITA. You mustn't think like that...

ALFRED. Why not? They ought to smash all those filthy shacks.

RITA. What would happen to the people?

ALFRED. They'd have to find somewhere else.

RITA. And the children?

ALFRED. Why should it matter where they live their worthless lives?

RITA. You're making yourself cruel, Alfred.

ALFRED. I *have* to be cruel now, it's my duty.

RITA. Your duty?

ALFRED. My duty to avenge Eyolf's death. It's got to be done, I'm telling you, think about it, you have to raze the whole place to the ground after I'm gone.

RITA. After you're gone?

ALFRED. It'll give you something to fill your life with and you're going to need that.

RITA. Can you guess what I will do… after you're gone?

ALFRED. What?

RITA (*slowly*). As soon as you're gone, I'll go down to the beach and bring all those children home with me. All those starving and wild and neglected boys and girls –

ALFRED. What will you do with them?

RITA. I'll take them to my heart.

ALFRED. You?

RITA. Yes, me. They'll all be here, all of them, as if they were my children.

ALFRED. In Eyolf's home?

RITA. Yes, in our little Eyolf's home. They'll live in his rooms. Read his books. Play with his toys. Take it in turns to sit in his place at meals.

ALFRED. This is insane. I don't know a single woman in the whole world less suited than you for a thing like that.

RITA. I'll have to educate myself for it. Teach myself. Train myself.

ALFRED. If you're really serious about this, really serious, then you must really have changed, you must have been transformed.

RITA. Yes I have been and I have you to thank for that. You've made me hollow and I have to try to fill up the empty space with something. With something that's a little like love.

ALFRED *moves a pace or two, then stands lost in thought, then looks at* RITA. *The light inside the house flickers and dies. They both turn to it.*

ALFRED. It's true, we haven't done much for the people down there.

RITA. We've done nothing for them.

ALFRED. We've scarcely thought of them.

RITA. Never sympathetically.

ALFRED. We had our 'burnished gold and great green forests' –

RITA. But our hands were closed to them. And our hearts.

ALFRED. No wonder they did nothing to save Eyolf.

RITA. Are you sure that... that we'd have risked our lives?

ALFRED. Of *course* we would.

RITA. We're not gods, Alfred, we're earthbound.

ALFRED. What do you really think you can do for these children?

RITA. I want to try to make their lives better, or at least less miserable.

ALFRED. If you can achieve that then Eyolf didn't live for nothing.

RITA. Or die for nothing, either.

ALFRED. It's not love that's driving you to do this, is it?

RITA. No, it isn't, at least not yet.

ALFRED. What is it then?

RITA *walks away from him.*

RITA. You used to talk so often to Asta about your book...

ALFRED....that you hated...

RITA. I still hate it, but I used to sit and listen to what you told her about human responsibility and now I'm going to try... in my own way... to put it into effect.

ALFRED. For the sake of a book I couldn't write?

RITA. No.

ALFRED. Then why?

RITA. I want to make my peace with the eyes that stare at me.

ALFRED. Do you think I might help?

RITA. Would you?

ALFRED. If I thought I could.

RITA. You'd have to stay here.

ALFRED. Let's see what we can do together.

RITA. Let's.

> ALFRED *moves to the table and turns off the lamp. It's dark now, just the stars above.*
>
> *Then he goes to* RITA, *stands close to her without touching.*

ALFRED. We've got a lot of work in front of us.

RITA. But every now and then we'll have earned a day of rest and feel at peace.

ALFRED. Then maybe we'll feel the presence of their spirits.

RITA. What spirits?

ALFRED. The ones we've lost.

RITA. Both Eyolfs.

ALFRED. Once in a while… we'll just have a small… passing… glimpse of them.

RITA. Where will we see them?

ALFRED. Above us.

RITA. Above us.

ALFRED. Towards the tops of the mountains. Towards the stars. Towards the great silence.

RITA *takes his hand. They stand together, motionless in the dark.*

RITA. Thank you.

The stars shine above them, then a shimmer of the aurora borealis.

www.nickhernbooks.co.uk

facebook.com/nickhernbooks

twitter.com/nickhernbooks